EXPLAINING
The Trinity

DAVID PAWSON

ANCHOR RECORDINGS

First published in Great Britain in 2016 by
Anchor Recordings Ltd
Synegis House, 21 Crockhamwell Road,
Woodley, Reading RG5 3LE

**For more of David Pawson's teaching,
including DVDs and CDs, go to
www.davidpawson.com**

**FOR FREE DOWNLOADS
www.davidpawson.org**

**For further information,
email: info@davidpawsonministry.com**

ISBN 978-1-911173-07-6

Printed by Lightning Source

Contents

This booklet is based on a talk. Originating as it does from the spoken word, its style will be found by many readers to be somewhat different from my usual written style. It is hoped that this will not detract from the substance of the biblical teaching found here.

As always, I ask the reader to compare everything I say or write with what is written in the Bible and, if at any point a conflict is found, always to rely upon the clear teaching of scripture.

David Pawson

David Rawson

Chapter One

THE DYNAMIC

The doctrine of the Trinity is under more attack today than perhaps it has ever been. To give you just two examples: Islam is opposing the doctrine of the Trinity and accusing us of worshipping three Gods. The fact that they think it is Father, Son and Virgin Mary is simply a naïve mistake. But they criticise severely Christians who are supposed to believe in three Gods. Another group, even in the Name of Jesus, is violently opposed to the Trinity and that is the Jehovah's Witnesses – and I have had their usual booklet on this accusing us of being heretics for believing that God is three in one.

I could go on – feminism is making a huge attack on the traditional doctrine of the Trinity, so much so that I have a book on my shelves called *The Battle for the Trinity* by Donald Bloesch, one of my favourite authors, and to my astonishment, it's pretty well all about feminism and feministic theology, and what is left of the Trinity after they have finished with it. So from all sides, the doctrine of the Trinity is under attack.

The difficulty is that the church is not in a position to defend it. I have met many pastors, clergy, who just don't like preaching on Trinity Sunday – it is the Sunday after Pentecost. So I am hoping to make you stronger and more able to defend the Trinity as you read this, because the only real defence against all this attack is that Christians think clearly about what they believe and are able to talk about it and defend "the faith once delivered to the saints", which scripture exhorts us to do.

In this first part, I want to talk about the Bible and how this doctrine grew out of the Bible as we have it. But in the second part, which will tax your brain a little more, I want to address the early centuries of the church and how they developed this. Some of our critics are very eager to point out that the word 'Trinity' is not in the Bible. They usually argue that it was invented as a doctrine later than Jesus, probably in the fourth century A.D. by Tertullian, as a shorter form of "triunity". Therefore I want to begin with the Bible and show you that this Bible of ours makes the problem quite acute. I call it a problem to begin with but I am hoping by the end of this chapter you will be rejoicing in the Trinity and thanking God for it, and not regarding it as an embarrassing thing to defend – not as a bit like Alice in Wonderland believing six impossible things before breakfast.

The Trinity is not given to us to argue about but I want to make a case for it. Let us start with the Old Testament which is three-quarters of your Bible and consists of Jewish scriptures; and one thing that we owe to the Jewish people is to believe in one God. Most nations in those days had many gods (what we call "polytheism" – poly– being "many", –theism being "gods"). Into that world, when everybody believed in many gods, came the Jews who believed in one. From the time of Abraham onwards, they believed in that one God. They believed they knew his Name. In Hebrew, the name of God is JHVH. The only trouble is that "j" is pronounced like a "y" and "v" like a "w". From those four letters, the British got "Jehovah" and that is still used in some of our hymns. But, as far as we know, the Hebrew word is *Yahweh*, using that y and w. I have tried the hardest I can to get a Jew to tell me how to say that word but they will not use it. They are so scared of taking the name of God in vain. I just say to one, "How do you pronounce that name for God?" They say, "Ya... No, you're not going to get me..." And they go no further than the "y".

So, monotheism we owe to the Jews and the nearest they have ever come to a creed is a verse from Deuteronomy chapter 6 which says "Hear O Israel: The LORD our God is one." That is the heart of the Jewish faith. That verse is probably the most important and the most widely used among them and I want to say a little about it before we move on. First: The word "Lord" is not in it. Wherever you see the word LORD in capital letters in the Old Testament, you know that is where the Name of God is, which they dare not say – Yahweh. So really it is "Hear O Israel: Yahweh our God is one."

The next thing I want to say about that is that the word "one" is important because there are two Hebrew words for one. One means singular – one single thing or person; but the other Hebrew word (*echad*) means "many but who are one in harmony in mind, one in thought". That is the word that is used in that verse: *echad*. So it does not mean that they believe in one singular God but it does mean that they believe in a harmonious God. That is a rather important point. The word "one" is used way back in Genesis for the married couple where the two become *one* flesh. They are still two persons but their flesh has become one, in harmony. It is not two separate individuals now, it is one. So they become "The Pawsons" or whatever – they are one couple. So even Deuteronomy chapter 6 needs to be read more carefully.

Now when you say you believe in one God, you are also saying you believe in the *only* God, one and only. That is drawn out in the prophet Isaiah, particularly in the latter chapters where again and again God says, 'There is no God

9

beside me.' He is the only God as well as the one God. Other countries had many gods, but Judaism had one and only. But there are hints all the way through the Old Testament of plurality in God as against singularity, and they are only hints in the Old Testament which many Jews have not noticed, and by which other Jews are left perplexed.

So what are these hints of plurality? One is that when God talks about himself, he calls himself "us". He does that right from the first page of Genesis when he said, "Let *us* make man in *our* own image." Now who is he talking to? Some Jews say he must have been talking to the angels but we are not made in the image of angels. Others say: well, the plural is the plural of majesty as when Queen Elizabeth gives her Christmas broadcast and says "we" instead of "I". Do you know why she does that? It is because she is speaking on behalf of all the kings and queens we have had. "We" – she is now representative of a long line of people, not just one person: "we" – the royal lines that have made our monarchy. But that is not true with God. God doesn't do it because of his majesty. He must be doing it because he is more than one. It is not just in Genesis 1, it is in Genesis 11 where he talks about the Tower of Babel and says, "Let *us* go down and see what man is doing." Supremely, in the call of Isaiah (Isaiah chapter 6) – "Whom shall *we* send and who will go for *us*?" Now that is just one of the suggestions in the Old Testament that, though they believed in one God, there was just a hint that he might be more than one. Jews have been puzzled by this.

The next thing I want to mention is that the word translated "God" is the Hebrew word *Elohim* and the intriguing thing about that is that it is a plural word. "El" is the word for one God. "Eloha" is the word for two. But *Elohim* is a word meaning more than two, and Elohim is used throughout the Old Testament for God. Again, many people who don't know Hebrew have not noticed that, and those who do have noticed it and been puzzled by it, but it is there, and it leads to some very odd grammar. The first verse in Genesis 1 reads like this: "In the beginning, Gods (*Elohim*) created". You get a grammatical error of a plural noun and a singular verb because the word "created" there is singular. That carries on right through the Old Testament: a plural word for God with singular verbs alongside it.

Looking back from a Christian point of view, that makes sense to us whilst It doesn't make sense to Jews. It is a grammatical mistake to use a plural noun and a singular verb. So there are all these complications in the Old Testament that give a hint of the Trinity as we know it. One of the most outstanding is this verse: "And the LORD [that is *Yahweh*] appeared to Abraham and he saw three men. Did you ever notice that? So the LORD's appearance to Abraham was in the form of three men.

That takes me back to one extraordinary occasion when Premier Radio asked me to take part in an experiment, which was to put two people together in the studio who had never met and who were as different as chalk and cheese, and let them get to know each other. They asked me to volunteer and I said okay, and when I was introduced to the man who I would get to know, his name was Chris Lambrianou, a Greek who had been a member of the Kray Brothers Gang in East London. You could not have had two more opposite people. But he had found Christ and, you know, within two minutes we were in brotherly love with each other. It was an extraordinary case and we couldn't have been more different – how we had been raised, our education or anything else. He was in prison for fifteen years, most of the time in solitary confinement, and he was suicidal. So he was in a cell with an iron bedstead cemented into the floor so he couldn't do anything damaging to himself. But he was in total despair and someone gave him a box of books. In the box was this book, and he thought: that's a Bible. I've heard that that does you good. So he decided to sleep on it. And he had the best night's sleep he had had in years. He thought: this is a great book – it does you so much good. He tucked it into his jerkin and walked around with it for a day. Then he got more and more interested because his life began to change. At last he decided to read it and he read about the Lord.

One night, he woke up in the early hours of the morning and there were three bearded men standing at the foot of his bunk. He said to them, "I know who you are, you're the Father, you're the Son and you're the Holy Spirit."

The middle one said, "Just follow Me, Chris."

From that day he gave his life to Christ and he is doing great work rescuing young men from the sort of life he'd had. So the judges in the court where he does this say to young men who have got into trouble, "I sentence you to live with Chris Lambrianou for twelve months." And at the end of twelve months, you can guess what the result has been.

Chris had a vision of the Lord – in total ignorance of the scripture or anything else, and he knew they were Father, Son and Holy Spirit. That is exactly what happened to Abraham. The Lord appeared to Abraham and he saw three men. Now we could go on like this but the Old Testament leaves us with two huge questions about two people. First, the Messiah (Greek: "the Christ"), and the Messiah is right through the Old Testament. There are hints about him all the way through. But the question we are left with is this: are they expecting a human or a divine Messiah? Some passages suggest human, some hint at divine. Only the New Testament gives the answer: both! But the Jews still argue about the Messiah, whether he is going to be a human like David or divine. In the book of Daniel, it sounds as if he is going to be divine, even though he is called the Son of Man. In other books, he is a great King. So that is one question that we are left with in the Old Testament.

The second question concerns the Holy Spirit. You can't decide when you read the Old Testament – is the Holy Spirit a thing or a person; an "it", or a "he"? There are many passages that speak of the Spirit of God as an "it", a kind of force emanating from God that can come on people. And there are other passages which talk about grieving the Holy Spirit. Now you can't grieve a thing, you can only cause grief to a person. So there is an ambiguity in the Old Testament.

Now all these things I have been telling you about are from the Old Testament, but can you see that they are all pointing to the New? In the New, the questions get answered and the things are brought together that are separate in the Old. But that is the Old Testament preparation for belief in the Trinity and it is there for eyes that are open to see.

Turning to the New Testament now, we find it is as strong as the Old that God is one – no change to that. In fact, at least five or six of the New Testament writers quote Deuteronomy 6:4 – "Hear O Israel: the LORD our God is one." Even Jesus himself quoted that verse. So there is no question about it that the God of the New Testament is as much one as the God of the Old Testament – no change. And though most of the writers of the New Testament are Jewish, they are not embarrassed to say that he is one. However, this is where the complication begins. They had met Jesus, and at first they could not work out who he was – what kind of a person he was. The Gospels faithfully record their perplexity. When he stilled the storm, they said, "What kind of a man is this, that even the wind and the waves obey him and do what he tells them?" What he told them, by the way, was not "Peace, be still." That is our polite modern version. What he actually said could be translated "Get muzzled!" – the order you give to a dog that is jumping up and messing our clothes: "Get down!" They said: what kind of a man is this? It took them two and a half years to find out.

Let us look at what we call the Synoptic Gospels first. Synoptic means "to look together": –optic, "to see"; syn– , "together". We call the first three Gospels synoptic because they are all looking from the same angle at Jesus – at what he said, what he did, and so on. Now the Synoptics are faithful to record that for two and a half years they just could not make him out. Everything he did puzzled them more. But at the same time he was healing people, raising the dead and casting out demons, and the demons knew who he was. It is there in the record that, again and again, when he battled with a demon who had taken possession of someone, the demon in the person would say, "I know who you are. You're the Holy One..." – you are this, that and the other. They were right. But Jesus, every time, said "shut up". He would say that – he wanted the disciples to come to their own convictions and not because the demons had said it. Demons are fallen angels – that is all they are. And they were, before anyone else, telling people who Jesus was. Have you ever noticed that? Jesus did not want demons telling his disciples or anyone else for that matter. He was waiting for someone to say, "I know who you are."

He took them to a place which is my favourite location in Israel. We have had the most amazing experiences there. It is at the foot of Mount Hermon, the big snow-capped mountain in the north of Israel. The snow melts and goes down inside a crack inside the mountain and comes out at the foot – a full-scale river. It appears to come straight out from a cliff, an amazing place. It is called Caesarea Philippi in your Bible. There, as you can imagine, were a lot of ideas as to who God was. To this day there are niches carved in the rock, which held statues. One of them was a Greek god called Pan. The place is still called Banias, after Pan, and he was a god who had appeared as a man in popular mythology. Another alcove had a statue of Caesar, hence the name Caesarea Philippi; Philip was the governor of the area. Caesar was a man whom people thought was a god. Jesus took his disciples one day to that very place where there was a statue of a god who appeared as a man and a man who was thought to be a god, and he said, "Who am I?" But he didn't say that first. His first question was, "Who do *people* say that I am?"

They replied: "You must be a reincarnation; you're such a great guy; and you're so young as well – you must be a reincarnation of a great man, maybe one of the prophets."

Jesus said: "But I have this question for you: 'Who do *you* think I am?'"

Peter said: "I know; you weren't born here, you came from somewhere else; you are the Son of the living God."

Jesus had been waiting two and a half years for just one person to guess who he was, and once they knew who he was, he could get on with what he had come to do, which was to die.

From that minute, he set his face to go to Jerusalem. He said: "Now I can be crucified."

Peter said, "You'll do no such thing," and argued with him, and Jesus had to say to one of his best friends, "Get behind me, Satan", meaning: you are not talking like God now; you are talking like Satan talks.

Now then, Peter was the first man to realise the truth. Do you know who was the first woman to make the same confession? Just turn a few pages over and you find that Martha, who was so busy in the kitchen, was the first to say, "You're the Son of the living God."

Now Jesus had what he needed, a man and a woman who realised who he was, and who would tell others who he was. So he could die for us, and very soon afterwards, that is exactly what he did.

He was very tender in the way he led the disciples to that realisation. They did not know then where he had been born. They thought it was Nazareth but it wasn't, it was Bethlehem. They did not know then how he was born because Mary had 'kept all these things in her heart' – didn't share them. They did not know anything about his boyhood at this stage, and as far as we can tell, they did not know anything about his baptism. But at all those three points his heavenly Father had a real part to play. And the word "Father" now comes right into general use. If there was one thing that Jesus did, it was to teach us to call God "Father". No Jew would ever do that. It would be presumptuous to call God your "Dad", because the word he gave us was "Abba", which was the first word a baby in a Jewish home learns when he sees that great monster leaning over the cot. He says "Abba" and the proud father says, "He called me, he knows me."

Jesus had such an intimate prayer life that they asked him, "Teach us to pray like you do."

He replied: when you pray, say "Abba"; come as a little child to God.

Looking back over the life of Jesus, his heavenly Father was there all the way through. I say his *heavenly* Father because he did not have an earthly one.

Only later did the stories of his birth come out. They were dug out by Matthew and Luke and they show that from the very beginning of his earthly life he had an earthly mother and a divine Father. From his conception onwards, his heavenly Father meant everything to him. He was there at the conception, he was there in the birth, he was there in his boyhood – that is a story alone; it is the only glimpse we have of his entire life up to the age of thirty. His parents took him up to the temple in Jerusalem for his Bar Mitzvah, when a Jewish boy becomes a Jewish man, takes responsibility for keeping the Law himself. Parents have that responsibility up to the Bar Mitzvah. They left Jerusalem. They used to walk their journeys, in those days, fifteen miles at a time – and what happened was this: the children walked with their mothers on the way there, and on the way back, they walked with their fathers. The boys were now men. The women always set off first and put up the tent and cooked the evening meal, and then the men came later and caught up and ate the meal.

Now they walked fifteen miles out of Jerusalem after taking Jesus there, and they did not notice that Jesus wasn't with them. Why not? Because Mary said in her mind: he will walk with the men now; he is a man now. And Joseph said: well, he is not my boy so he will stay with Mary. So you can understand how they both walked fifteen miles and then discovered no Jesus. You know the rest of the story. They went back to Jerusalem, searched everywhere but the right place and finally said: shall we try the temple? And there he was, talking with the priests. Mary said an interesting thing: "Jesus, where have you been? Your father and I have been looking everywhere for you." It means that she had never told Jesus who his Father was. She had kept it in her heart, secret. Amazing! But it means that at maybe twelve or thirteen years of age he knew who his Father was. He said: but surely you know that when a boy has his Bar Mitzvah, he becomes a partner with his father in the family business; that is where you should have looked first for me. Didn't you realise I have now come into the Father's business? It all makes sense, doesn't it, when you see the truth of it? Of course, it wasn't known to the disciples, even that boyhood.

Then look at his baptism. The Father took part in that baptism. There was a voice from heaven, "This is my beloved Son in whom I am well pleased" – and the people said, it was thundering. When God actually speaks out loud, it is like a thunderstorm. If your ears are not tuned, you may

ear the actual words. But some people did, and that is
hey heard the Father say. This goes on all through his
ministry. He says: my miracles I'm doing are by the Spirit
of God, and he kept talking about Father but he never said,
'Our Father'. He told *us* to say that but he couldn't say it
himself. For himself, he always spoke of 'My Father' and
'Your Father'. He made that very careful distinction because
he was claiming to be *the* Son of God. That is what they were
coming to realise. This is *the Son*, and as soon as you say
the something, you are saying there is nobody else. When
he said, 'I am *the* Way, *the* Truth and *the* Life' – there is no
other way; there is no other truth; there is no other life. I'm
it! All this comes out clearly in the Synoptic Gospels.

His trial – he was condemned to death for blasphemy.
Now of course, the Romans couldn't crucify anyone without
a charge on the Roman law books, and blasphemy was not
on their books, so when they took Jesus to Pilate, they had
to change the charge to treason. In the Jewish court, he says
he is *the* Son of God. That was enough – blasphemy. But in a
Roman court, they said he is *the* king of the Jews – treason.
So Jesus is actually condemned to death for blasphemy
but the Roman charge was treason, and he was put to
death. On the cross he was for the first time ever separated
from his Father. That is why he cried out "Eloi, Eloi, lama
sabachthani" – my God, my God, why have you left me? It
is the cry of someone who had never known separation from
his Father. We need to get into the heart of Jesus.

So that was how the disciples came to recognise that he
was the Son of God. But wait, the one proof they needed
was yet to come. They confessed it now, they said it, but
something was going to happen that would settle it in their
minds forever. He was put to death for blasphemy and three
days later he was out of the tomb. That means that God had
reversed the verdict of the human court. The resurrection

was God saying: you were wrong; he was speaking the truth; he wasn't blaspheming when he claimed to be my Son; that was the truth – he was innocent, and you have convicted him wrongly. That is what the resurrection said to the disciples, and it was from that moment that they were absolutely sure that Jesus was *the* Son of God. Paul says at the beginning of Romans that he "was declared to be the Son of God, by his resurrection from the dead." It was God saying: that is my verdict.

So far I have not even touched on John's Gospel. When we turn to that, the whole Gospel is about one thing: that Jesus was, is, and always will be, *the* Son of God. Right from the beginning, he had a new name for Jesus because Jesus only got that name when he was a human being. But he had existed long before – forever before. So John gave him the name "Logos". The term was used by a man from Ephesus. "Logos" means "the reason why" and It was coined by a man called Heraclitus who was a famous scientist – one of the first. He said that the logos is the reason why things behave as they do. So, many branches of study at university are called an "-ology". Zoology is the study of why animals behave as they do; meteorology is the study of why weather behaves as it does; psychology is why the human mind behaves as it does; sociology is why human society behaves as it does. Every '-ology' is the reason why something happens, and it was surely the inspired move of God to John – the fourth Gospel – to call Jesus "the Logos", the reason why everything is. He is the Reason Why. And he says in the very first verse of John's Gospel: the Logos was with God (actually face to face with God) and the Logos *was* God. John's Gospel begins and ends with people calling Jesus God. If you have read my book *Unlocking the Bible* you will know that there are three sevens in John's Gospel: seven miracles, seven claims and seven witnesses.

Let us run quickly through them. There are seven miracles in John, five of which are not in the Synoptics and they are all more startling miracles, more divine miracles. He does not call them miracles, he calls them signs. And each miracle he did was a sign pointing to God – changing water into wine. The Synoptics never noticed that, but John did because it was a sign pointing to the Creator. Healing a man who had been forty years blind – a long time. Raising Lazarus after four days when his body was putrid and stinking, and he raised Lazarus. That was a God miracle, a God-like act. So there are seven miracles, all signs, pointing to Jesus as God. Then there were seven witnesses who called him God, beginning with John himself in the Gospel – "the Word was God", ending with Thomas, the doubting disciple who was the first to say "My Lord and My God". He was Jewish yet he was saying that without embarrassment, without difficulty, spontaneously recognising the Lord's divinity.

The only two miracles that repeat the Synoptics are walking on water and feeding five thousand people with a couple of fish and a few loaves of bread. All of them are such divine miracles that they are signs pointing towards who did them.

Then there are seven words from Jesus, seven claims, each of which began with 'Yahweh' because we know the meaning of it – it is "I Am what I Am"; "I Am the Great I Am." Even in Greek, it is: "I, I am" – *ego eimi*, and *eimi* means "I am" but *ego* means "I" so that a real translation of these seven claims would be "I, I am...." It begins with the Bread of Heaven. It goes on through so many other things – seven things Jesus claimed: the Good Shepherd, The Door, The Way, the Truth, the Life, and so on.

So: seven miracles, seven witnesses and seven claims to be "I Am". Now you couldn't have much more than that. John's Gospel makes it quite clear, and when you get to the end of John's Gospel, he says, "If everything Jesus said and did was written down, the world couldn't contain the books, but these have been written so that you may go on believing that Jesus is *the* Son of God." That is why John wrote the Gospel. He had been closer to Jesus than anybody else, and he had been longer with Jesus because all the other twelve apostles had been killed. He was the only one who died of old age. And he was the one to look after Mary, the mother of Jesus. Jesus knew that all the others were to be killed so he gave his mother to the care of John, the beloved disciple, who always sat next to Jesus when they sat for a meal, and he was surely the one to know what kind of a man this was.

Now I present all this to you because, with the Gospels alone, they have a problem and the problem was they had met two persons they called God. As Jews, they knew about God in heaven, the God who had brought them out of Egypt. They knew *that* God, but now they have got a problem. Jesus is God too. They always felt that he was the same in nature and attitude and every other way, so much so that when he said "If you have seen me, you've seen the Father" they just took that as truth. They knew they could see what God was like in Jesus, so if that was the end of the story we wouldn't be Trinitarians, we would be "binitarians", we would believe in Two-in-One God. But it wasn't the end of the story. They were going to meet a third person who was God and who was the same God as the other two – exactly the same.

So let us go on to someone else: the Holy Spirit. Now you remember I told you that in the Old Testament they could not decide whether the Spirit of God was a thing or a person, and the same kind of ambiguity goes into the New Testament because the Spirit in the New Testament is likened to wind and to water. That means they had an pneumatic expression for him and an aquatic one – wind and water. Those are things. Ah, but John's Gospel takes it much further than that. In John 14 to 16, on the last night of his life before he died, Jesus told them about the Holy Spirit and called him "he", not "it", and he said, "He will be another Comforter to you", and the Greeks have two words for "another". One is "another like" something, and the other word means "another unlike" something, but it is the word "like" something that he uses here – "another Comforter just like me; what I have been to you, he will be to you. In fact, he can't come and be with you until I go". All this points to what we call the *personality* of the Holy Spirit. And he is going to be just like Jesus to the disciples, another person just like him. It is from John's Gospel again that we get the message about the personality of the Holy Spirit.

Putting all this together, they have now met three persons, each of whom they have called God, each of whom is a real person to them, and yet it is the same God – exactly the same. Whether you are talking to one or the other, you gather this impression you are talking to the same person. They have exactly the same attitude to you, exactly the same care for you. Here are Jews who have met three persons whom they all know are divine and personal. Yet they are still Jews believing in one God. There you have got it. We have not even touched the rest of the New Testament yet but already we have found a solid basis for believing in the Three in One God – which is exactly who the Trinity is.

We come to the apostles and the epistles – the rest of the New Testament. They are all absolutely clear that God is one. They even quote Deuteronomy 6:4 again. Five of them do that. We are in the New Testament now, and the New Testament says that God is One. But they also confirm, firstly, that Jesus is divine and they attribute to him the three functions that only God has – creation, salvation and judgment. Those are three things that only God does, yet the epistles attribute to Jesus all those three functions. That is not a coincidence. Furthermore, they all take Old Testament concepts of God the Father and apply them to God the Son. God the Father was the first and the last, the beginning and the end – so is Jesus. There are at least ten attributes of God the Father in the Old Testament that the apostles applied to Jesus in the New. He is now the Light of the World.

Let us go on from there. They all in the epistles acknowledge the personality of the Holy Spirit, so that raises a problem. They begin to talk in terms of three. I'm going to mention two passages to illustrate that. The first is in Ephesians chapter 4: "Make every effort to keep the unity of the Spirit through the bond of peace. There is one Body and one Spirit – just as you were called to one hope when you were called – one Lord, one faith, one baptism; one God and Father of all, who is over all and through all and in all." Do you notice the three-fold one Spirit, one Christ, one God. It has almost become natural to them to think in terms of those three in one. Here is the other passage: 1 Corinthians 12, where Paul is talking about the gifts of the Spirit: "There are different kinds of gifts, but the same Spirit. There are different kinds of service, but the same Lord. There are different kinds of working, but the same God works all of them in all men." Do you notice that? The same Lord, the same Spirit, the same God. In 2 Corinthians: "May the grace of the Lord Jesus Christ and the love of God and the fellowship of the Holy Spirit be with you all."

Now that goes through all the epistles. They put Father, Son and Holy Spirit together on an equality; they make no difference between them – and they use that threefold formula to bless people. Even more than that, there is evidence that they worshipped Father, Son and Holy Spirit; as well as the benediction I have mentioned. What I have been trying to do is to give you a feel of how the Trinity inevitably emerged from the *experience* of the disciples.

Therefore they automatically thought in eternity of God in three persons. They didn't use the word 'Trinity' yet – I will tell you how that came about in the next chapter – but they were already thinking in terms of a triad. There are many different words they used, but they were threefold in their thinking and that is the heart of the doctrine.

Chapter Two

THE DOCTRINE

Inevitably, the Christian faith is going to be attacked in a fallen world. This is the Devil's kingdom according to my New Testament. "We know that we are of Christ, but we also know that the whole world is in the grip of the evil one." We are told every day to pray to be delivered from the evil one – that is the real version of the Lord's Prayer, not "...from evil" but "...from the evil one", the Devil. So the Lord's Prayer (as we call it) begins with "Father in heaven" but it ends with the Devil on earth. The two ways in which he attacks are these: he will attack the messengers of the gospel and the message of the gospel. He attacks the messengers by trying to get them to misbehave, to let the side down, to disobey God, not to follow his will. But that is another story and I am sure you have heard plenty of teaching on that. The two biggest dangers in that area are for the messengers to fall into license and do what they want, or into legalism and over-emphasise the Law of God. I have seen churches that have done both. Some churches go into license – don't care what their members do; and other churches go into legalism, and either way, you kill the life of the church.

But we are concerned here with the message and how the Devil seeks to pervert it and to spoil the gospel. We have seen how the gospel depends on Jesus being both fully human and fully divine – and the Devil wants to spoil one or the other. One of the first attacks he made on the Christian faith we call Docetism, which simply means not believing that Jesus came in flesh like ours but that he *appeared* as a kind of phantom or angel. And, yes, there are still people who think that Jesus was not real. Even today, people deny his existence though there are very few who do that. Even in the New Testament days, people were attacking his humanity, which is why John, in two of his three letters, said if a person doesn't believe that Jesus came in the flesh they are not a Christian. We need to believe in the real humanity of Jesus.

Now believers have a problem with Jesus' humanity. Unbelievers – their problem is with his divinity. But we are so used to worshipping Jesus, seeing him in a stained-glass window, that we forget that he was really human. The disciples were not among those who doubted Jesus' humanity. They had lived with it. They had eaten with him, they had slept in the same places, they had walked with him, they had talked with him. They knew Jesus was real and that he was fully human, and to them it was astonishing that some people had difficulty with that. But we have difficulty with it. I have mentioned before that Jesus had to empty his bowels and bladder every day just like we do. You never hear that talked about in church or even imagined, and yet Jesus talked about it. He was a real human being just like us, and one of the ways in which the Devil tries to destroy the Christian message is to convince people that Jesus wasn't real, that he wasn't fully human, that he was a heavenly visitor, a phantom, a ghost.

But the main attack that he makes is on the divinity of Jesus because that, after all, is the key. That is who he was, and it is only when they realised who he was that he went to Jerusalem to die. Because only then would people understand what was happening and what he was achieving. So the Devil attacks us morally and mentally, and it is the mental attack that I am concerned with now. I have shown you that John's Gospel was written almost entirely to support the deity of Jesus, that he was the Son of God. That is because John lived in Ephesus, where he looked after Mary, the mother of Jesus, for the rest of her life. But in Ephesus, there was a man called Cerinthus, and he said that Jesus was not fully divine, not fully human, that he was somewhere in between the two; that he could mediate on our behalf because he was between us and God, but he was not fully God. Now John knew about this. One day, John was taken to the public baths for a wash and he was in the water and he spotted Cerinthus at the other end of the Roman baths and shouted to his friends, "Get me out of here, get me out of here." They thought something was terribly wrong. He said, "I don't want to be in the same water as that man." He took a strong stand against him in this because there is nothing more damaging than to say Jesus was not fully divine, just a little less than God, somewhere in between.

Today, we have Jehovah's Witnesses saying that Jesus is not God and they argue, especially from their own bible which has been skilfully adjusted to fit their views. They don't believe that Jesus was God. They believe that he was a creature rather than the Creator, that he was the firstborn of all creation – that is one of the phrases they use, and it is biblical, but that he was formed first, however long ago; he was a creature. To say that "all things were made by him and through him and without him was not anything made that has been made" – that is blasphemy to Jehovah's Witnesses.

It is really about that divinity of Jesus that I am going to take a huge step now. At some point, somebody had a great idea: he said that what we need is a brief, concise statement of faith so that we can defend it against these who attack it. That is how creeds were formed (creed, from the latin word *credo* which means "I believe". The very first creed, put together by whom we don't know, is the Apostles' Creed which, if you are Anglican, is used every week in church. The Creeds were written to defend the faith against those who would deny it in some way. When you read it, ask: what was the attack this was defending the faith against? Because that is why they were written. So here is the Apostles' Creed, one of the earliest. Look at it and ask yourself what was being denied by the attackers.

I believe in God, the Father Almighty, creator of heaven and earth and I believe in Jesus Christ, his only Son, our Lord. He was conceived by the power of the Holy Spirit, born of the Virgin Mary, he suffered under Pontius Pilate, was crucified, died, and was buried. He descended to the dead. On the third day he rose again. He ascended into heaven and is seated at the right hand of the Father. He will come again to judge the living and the dead. I believe in the Holy Spirit, the holy catholic church, the communion of saints, the forgiveness of sins, the resurrection of the body and the life everlasting. Amen.

Are you familiar with those words? What was being said which that was written against? It may surprise you that the first point I want to make is this: it was written to defend his *humanity*; that people were already not believing that he was really human. Now why do I dare say that? Because it mentions his birth and his death. Furthermore, there are two human beings mentioned in the Apostles' Creed: Mary the mother of Jesus, and Pontius Pilate under whom he died. So this creed is saying he was born and he died, which are the two basic facts of every human being who has ever lived. They probably might go on your gravestone: you were born and you died, you are human.

So the first thing we say is that this was written to defend the full humanity of Jesus. That is why Pontius Pilate went down into history – because he was responsible for the death. Now you notice that we changed the word "hell" to the word "dead"; "he descended to the dead". That is a better translation because it is really "he descended into Hades", and when the creed was written, they were not clear as to whether hell and Hades were the same place or different places. But it means he descended to the dead. The other phrase we can misunderstand is "the holy catholic church". The word "catholic" meant – and means – "universal". It does not mean the church of Rome, and when this creed was written the holy catholic church was the holy universal church of all believers. So there is no problem with that.

But there is also a claim to facts of divine interruption in his life. Yes, he was born of Mary but he was conceived by the Holy Ghost, and therefore God was his Father. And yes, he was crucified under Pontius Pilate, but he was raised – on the third day he rose from the dead. Again, God is in there. So, while it is emphasising his true humanity, it is also emphasising the Fatherhood of God and all that God did to make Jesus possible.

Now I move from that creed, which was one of the earliest, to a creed that was formed at a place called Nicaea and it is called the Nicene Creed, which, if you are Anglican you would recite at a Communion Service. It is rather longer and it was written to defend the church's belief in Jesus' full divinity, because there was a man at that time called Arius and he was again one of those who claimed that Jesus was a creature rather than Creator and was somewhere in between God and man, but was not fully God. Now, in the light of that, consider the wording:

"We believe" (in modern translation; different from the

Apostles' Creed "I believe") in one God, the Father, the Almighty, Maker of heaven and earth and all that is, seen and unseen. We believe in one Lord Jesus Christ, the only Son of God, eternally begotten of the Father, God from God, Light from Light, true God from true God, begotten, not made, of one Being with the Father; through him, all things were made."

Now that is an amazing claim. You see what it is saying: Jesus was eternally begotten. That kills the idea of him being a creature. In other words, "begotten" does not mean that God *made* him. He was *eternally begotten* of the Father. He always was the Son of God. He did not *become* the Son of God. And he was true God from true God. One version is: "Very God from Very God". That is really emphasising he was *fully God* and you must not question that. "Of one being with the Father" – that is all of a piece with the same thing. "Through him all things were made" – a quote from John's Gospel, but it's saying he was not a creature; he was the Creator, as the New Testament frequently says. So it goes on: "For us and for our salvation, he came down from heaven .... By the power of the Holy Spirit he became incarnate..." – there is a word that is not in the Bible: incarnate. It means "enfleshed" – that he was made in carnal flesh. So somebody had begun to deny the incarnation – "became incarnate from the Virgin Mary and was made man. For our sake, he was crucified under Pontius Pilate, he suffered death and was buried. On the third day, he rose again in accordance with the Scriptures; he ascended into heaven, he is seated at the right hand of the Father. He will come again in glory to judge the living and the dead, and his Kingdom will have no end." There is an addition, so some people were already teaching that Jesus' kingdom was not everlasting.

Do you begin to see how you should read the creeds? You ask of every statement: what is it denying? And that is what was being said, and this was the church's response. "We believe in the Holy Spirit, the Lord, the Giver of Life, who proceeds from the Father and the Son." That is new. And that is one of the early controversies – who sent the Holy Spirit? There were some saying God did, and God alone; and others were saying that God the Father and God the Son sent the Spirit together, which is more in line with scripture again. "With the Father and the Son he is worshipped and glorified. He has spoken through the prophets. We believe in one holy catholic and apostolic church." There is an additional word there now: "apostolic". "We acknowledge one baptism for the forgiveness of sins." That is a new thing – "baptism" was not in the Apostles' Creed. "We look for the resurrection of the dead, and the life of the world to come." There was a controversy about baptism already coming in, perhaps because it was already being applied to babies.

The next creed I want to mention was written about A.D. 400 and it was named after a great defender of the Trinity named Athanasius, and is called the Athanasian Creed. He was particularly concerned about the people teaching that there were three Gods, not one. I think this creed rather overdoes it but listen to it:

"This is what the catholic faith teaches. We worship one God in the Trinity and Trinity in Unity. We distinguish among the Persons but we do not divide the substance for the Father is a distinct Person, the Son is a distinct Person and the Holy Spirit is a distinct Person. Still, the Father and the Son and the Holy Spirit have one Divinity, equal glory, and co-eternal majesty. What the Father is, the Son is, and the Holy Spirit is. The Father is uncreated, the Son is uncreated and the Holy Spirit is uncreated. The Father is boundless, the Son is boundless and the Holy Spirit is boundless. The Father is eternal, the Son is eternal and the Holy Spirit is eternal."

And we're only a third of the way through all this, by

the way.

"Nevertheless, they are not three eternal Beings, but one eternal Being. Thus there are not three uncreated Beings, not three boundless Beings, but one uncreated Being and one boundless Being. Likewise, the Father is omnipotent, the Son is omnipotent and the Holy Spirit is omnipotent yet there are not three omnipotent Beings but one omnipotent Being. Thus the Father is God, the Son is God and the Holy Spirit is God but there are not three Gods, but one God. The Father is Lord, the Son is Lord and the Holy Spirit is Lord. There are not three Lords but one Lord, for according to creation truth, we must profess that each of the Persons individually is God and according to Christian religion, we are forbidden to say there are three Gods or three Lords. The Father is made of none, neither created nor begotten, the Son of the Father alone not made nor created but begotten. The Holy Spirit is of the Father and of the Son, neither made nor created nor begotten but proceeding. So there is one Father, not three Fathers, one Son, not three Sons, one Holy Spirit, not three Holy Spirits and in this Trinity, none is before nor after another, none is greater or less than another but the whole three Persons are co-eternal and co-equal so that in all things as aforesaid the Unity in Trinity and the Trinity in Unity is to be worshipped."

I think he has made his point. But the church was so anxious to keep the faith on track and in this case they were so anxious not to divide God into three, which again can easily be done. They are not the same Person but they are the same God. This is the most difficult part for us to grasp, but we will come back to that in a moment.

One more creed is called the Chalcedonian Creed because of where it was written in A.D. 451. Now, again, consider: what is this denying?

"Therefore following the holy fathers, we all with one

accord teach men to acknowledge one and the same Son, our Lord Jesus Christ, at once complete in Godhead and complete in manhood, truly God and truly Man, consisting also of a reasonable soul and body, of one substance with the Father as regards his Godhead and at the same time of one substance with us as regards his manhood. Like us in all respects apart from sin. As regards his Godhead, begotten of the Father before the ages but yet as regards his manhood, begotten for us men and for our salvation, of Mary the Virgin, the God-bearer. One and the same Christ, Son, Lord, Only-begotten, recognized in two natures without confusion, without change, without division, without separation, the distinction in natures being in no way annulled by the union but rather characteristics of each nature being preserved and coming together to form one Person and subsistence not as parted or separated into two Persons but one and the same Son and only begotten God, the Word, Lord Jesus Christ even as the prophets from earlier times spoke of him and our Lord Jesus Christ himself taught us and the creeds of the fathers as handed down to us."

There is a concern here, not about the Holy Spirit yet, but about the Son, that there were two natures brought together in perfect harmony, the divine and the human combined in Christ.

Now those are all the creeds we are going to think about here, but they were all written to defend the faith and keep it pure and I am grateful to those who worked at it. Don't go along with everything they said – they are not infallible; they are not Scripture and we must not treat them as Scripture. There are some things, for example, that they say that I have problems with. One of the last that I read called Mary "the God bearer". Did you notice that? *Theotokos* is the Greek word, and unfortunately people got hold of that and began to talk about Mary as the mother of God. Have you heard that? Catholics now believe that as dogma. She was not the mother of God. She never was the mother of God. She was the mother of God's Son. She was not the mother of God. That puts her above God and is one of the reasons why Catholics have such a veneration for Mary the mother of God. But she was the mother of the Son, the mother of one of the three Persons, but not of the other two. She was not the mother of the Holy Spirit; she was not the mother of God the Father, so we need to again realise the creed didn't claim that she was mother of God, but that she was a God-bearer, and that is true. When you turn that into mother of God, it has gone too far.

After those creeds, there are still huge issues that theologians have to tackle and which they are still tackling. The first is: is there any order? How do they relate to each other? Is there a subordination? Feminist theologians categorically deny that, but there is an order. The Father *sent* the Son; the Son and the Father *sent* the Spirit; nobody sent the Father. It is a word that is never used of the Father. Jesus came to do his Father's will. He did it voluntarily, perfectly; but he came to glorify the Father. The Holy Spirit came to glorify the Son, and they don't glorify the other way, though the Son did pray, "Father, glorify me with the glory I had at the beginning." But there does seem an order, and in every creed there were always three sections and they were always in the order: Father, Son, Holy Spirit. In other words, the Father has the priority. His will is the basic that the other two do. So there is a certain order there, a certain subordination of a voluntary kind, which raised the second issue: are they equal? The answer is they are subordinate in some ways and equal in others. They are equal in glory, equal in status, equal in so many ways, but there is an order there. Then came another big question: How long has God been three? There are some even today who say he became three Persons in order to save us. That is called the Economic Theory of the Trinity. But the final answer of Christians has been: they were *always* Father, Son and Holy Spirit.

It is at this point that your brains begin to stretch a bit – they certainly do. Let us come to modern errors, which do suggest that we might need modern creeds to come to modern errors. There are still churches that cannot accept that God is three Persons. We call them Unitarian churches, and America is full of them. They worship one God but they do not include the Trinity. They talk about Jesus, they talk about the Holy Spirit. So do the Jehovah's Witnesses. But the Trinity is still anathema. There is a group of Pentecostals called the Oneness Pentecostal. Have you heard of them? Again, America seems to have produced these things, and the Oneness Pentecostals believe that God is one and that Jesus and the Holy Spirit are just the one God, which frankly means that God the Father died on the cross for you. That has been a well-known error for centuries. The Father didn't die on the cross. It was the Son who died on the cross. Father deserted his Son because he was making him to be sin on our behalf (see 2 Corinthians 5:21). But the error has been exposed as Patripassionism (sorry for these long words; "patri-", Father; "passion", suffers). People can still, without thinking, talk like that, but it is not the truth.

I have mentioned Jehovah's Witnesses, I have mentioned feminists, and the feminists make a big attack on the Trinity. They cannot bear the thought that anybody is subordinate to anybody else, that anybody is under someone else's will, and there are obvious reasons why they believe that. But to apply it to God is a mistake because it is from God, as I am going to show you in a moment, that we get our pattern.

I am going to suggest something here that I ask you to think about carefully. I believe many Evangelicals are Trinitarian in theory but in practice are Binitarian. You have been in churches where the Trinity seems to be in practice: Father, Son and Holy Scripture. Do you know what I mean? You will not hear much talk about the Holy Spirit in such churches, and they believe that the gifts and the Spirit ceased two thousand years ago when the scripture was complete. I think I don't need to say more. Nevertheless, in practice that is anti-Trinitarian. It may not be in theory, but in practice you will hear a lot of talk about the Father and about the Son and about the Holy Scripture, but very little about the Holy Spirit. I say that advisedly. I don't want the question to be objectively critical but I used to be that sort of Evangelical, and I dreaded preaching on Pentecost Sunday. I was always glad to get back to the gospel the next week and I could get enough out of books to make two sermons on Pentecost Sunday, but that is all it was. And for the rest, I confess that I could preach many, many sermons and never mention him. That is a very subtle form of what I call "Binitarianism". It means that many people in such churches don't know the Holy Spirit as a Person, they don't know him to talk to him, or they don't know him to listen to. I believe that I am a Charismatic Evangelical. In other words, I believe we need the Holy Spirit, and the Father and the Son, and that we need all three together, as the Holy Scripture tells us.

So let me come to today. How are we going to explain all this to people? Think of some mathematical equations. The first equation is one that many people think we believe and teach, and they can't understand why we don't believe in three gods, for then the mathematics of it are: $1+1+1=3$. But I would submit there is another mathematical equation that is nearer the truth: $1 \times 1 \times 1 = 1$. God is not tied to mathematics but I just give you that in case you want another mathematical formula that makes more sense when you talk about the Trinity. Just change "plus" to "times" and you are in a whole different world.

Some people want symbols. In many churches you see a symbol in the architecture or carved in wood at the end of the pew, that is always a symbol of the Trinity. When Patrick, the Welsh boy who was a slave, went to evangelise Ireland, he used the shamrock, and it has become the Irish national plant. He said: is that one leaf or three? It has three lobes but it only has one stem so is that one leaf or three? And he used the shamrock as a kind of symbol of the Trinity to help people to understand.

I think analogies don't help at all. I had a Professor at Cambridge who said, I want you to think of three eggs in a frying pan and the whites have flowed into one but there are three yolks. He said: that's a picture of the Trinity. Well, God is not eggs in a frying pan. But all such analogies fall down. A favourite analogy is water, H_2O, which can be steam, water or ice – a vapour, a liquid or a solid. I have heard that used as an argument. But, again, it breaks down because water can never be all three at the same time. It will either change into ice or change into steam, it is never ice, water and steam together. So it is not an analogy. So I really say: forget analogies.

I have one illustration which I have found helpful which is a triangle with Father at the top, Son at one apex and Spirit at another, and then there are various lines connecting them. A long line on the outside is a line that says "is not" – so the Father is not the Spirit, the Father is not the Son; the Son is not the Spirit. But in the middle of the diagram is the word 'God' and shorter lines connect the three to the centre and the shorter line says "is, is, is" – the Father *is* God, the Son *is* God, and the Spirit *is* God. They are different from each other, but they are all God. Now that does not argue anything but I felt it a helpful diagram to keep in my mind. It keeps me orthodox and it says something to my mind that I need to remember.

But let us move on. I think the most important thing I want to say now is this: *dynamic precedes doctrine – experience comes before explanation.* That was how it was in the Bible days. It was because they experienced the dynamic of the Trinity and had to work out the doctrine. That is the order, and therefore I say earnestly to you: don't try and explain the Trinity to an unbeliever. Tell them about the dynamic first; introduce them to the threefold relationship first. Don't try and argue them into believing in the Trinity until they have met all three Persons. Therefore, with unbelievers, I beg you: don't waste your time arguing about the Trinity. Preach the gospel to them; introduce them to all three Persons, then you are not going to have any difficulty telling them they have met the same God in all three. So that is the first practical application of all we have been learning. Don't try and convince unbelievers of the Trinity. You will never make it. They will tie you up in knots before you get anywhere. Introduce them to the *experience* of the Trinity and then they will be ready to listen to the doctrine. And they need to hear the doctrine but only after they have experienced three relationships – and I mean all three.

They need to be introduced to the Father, to the Son and to the Holy Spirit from the very beginning of their Christian life. Too many have to wait years before they are introduced to the Holy Spirit as a personal relationship. We only know the Father through the Son and "no man comes to the Father except through the Son", and those are the first two that most Christians are introduced to. But why aren't they introduced to the Holy Spirit as well? Because when they are baptised, which should come early in their Christian life, they will be baptised in the Name of the Father, the Son and the Holy Spirit. How can they be baptised into the name of a Person they don't know? Now, of course, here we have a problem. Jesus himself said, Go and make disciples of all the nations, baptising them in the Name of *the* Father and *the* Son and *the* Spirit. And the word "the" is very important because that is what makes it a Person.

We don't have a threefold name for God – Father, Son and Holy Spirit – as if that is his name. His name is *the* Father, *the* Son and *the* Spirit, and that makes sure you are treating them as separate Persons, different from each other. Now the problem is that the name in there is singular, and here again we have a grammatical conundrum. The single name of *the* Father, *the* Son and *the* Holy Spirit, the single name of three Persons, is a contradiction grammatically and mathematically, but it is the truth. So I believe our basic task is to introduce people to all three; if necessary, one by one, but hopefully as close together as possible so that they have met and know all three and yet they will know instinctively that they are dealing with the same God in all three.

Now I come to the most important thing. Let me put this very carefully. The real answer to the conundrum of the Trinity is to ask: in what sense is God three, and in what sense is he one? Don't ever confuse those two things. There are some senses in which God is three and other senses in which God is one, but the two are different and must never be the same. Let us ask first about the three. God is three Persons. The Father is not the Son and is not the Spirit. His Threeness is Persons. He is not one Person. Do you follow me? If only we had not allowed our minds to slip into thinking that he was three Persons and one Person at the same time. That is where we make the problem for people. He is three Persons but one God. So what he is as three is different from what he is as one. Now I hope you follow me in that, because then it is no longer a problem. He is only three in some senses and only one in entirely different senses. You are not asking that the three and the one be applied to the same thing. That is when you are into contradiction and mathematical nonsense.

So, get this clearly: the three only applies to three Persons. The problem then is of course: in what sense are the three one? Not in personhood. We know what a person is. I am a person, you are a person, I am not you, you are not me, we are different. So how do we get the oneness? There is only one human analogy that helps and that is sexual intercourse. Now that is the analogy that the Bible uses – when two become one flesh, and we can use that analogy. It only goes as far as getting two into one, but at least we can say God is one step beyond that. He is three into one. You know Jesus said, quite specifically, "I and the Father are one", but he did not mean one Person. He meant two in perfect harmony, sharing the same nature, the same attitudes, the same attributes. Three share one nature, not one Person. The three Persons are in total harmony.

Let me finish by asking: what is the importance of all this? What is the relevance of all this? Isn't the Trinity just a theory, and how does it impact my daily life? Well, the crucial question in all religion is: what kind of God do you believe in? That is going to affect everything else.

Let us take Islam. They don't believe in a Trinity. They believe in one person called god. We believe in three Persons. What difference does that make? Quite simply, for us, God is above us, beside us and within us. God the Father is above us, so we can worship a God in heaven. But he became Immanuel, God *with* us, God beside us, God sharing our nature. And when you have been filled with the Holy Spirit, you know that God is within you. Now if you over-emphasise any of those three, you come to an unbalanced view of God. Islam over-emphasises the god above us, and that is all they have; but we have a God who came beside us and said: I will send you another Standby. That's what the word Comforter means there – Standby. I will send you another Standby and he will be within you. So if you ask, where is my God? He is above me, he is beside me, he is in me. And that is my whole being covered, my whole existence is in God and I have got the God I need. I need a God who is above me. I need a God who is beside me. I need a God who is within me. That is the three dimensions of my life, and God fills all three, and only God the Trinity does that. Allah can't do that. There is no claim in the Koran that he can. He can't. He will always be a solitary person above them and you can't have that "beside" or "inside" relationship with him.

But "Immanuel" means "God with us, God beside us", and the Holy Spirit meant "God within me". Now if you over-emphasise God within you, you reduce him in size. He becomes a little God in your heart. Or you can over-emphasise that in Christ he became beside us – and miss out on the within. The Christian alone, of all the religions in the world, can boast of a God above us, beside us and within us. Now that is the most important fact of the Trinity, and if you don't believe in the Trinity, you will lose at least one or two of those three things and that would be a tragedy.

What does this mean for God? It means that God is *relational*. God has relations within himself and therefore only Christianity can ever say – and it is the only religion that has said – God is Love, because you can't have love with a solitary person. Love is a relationship and therefore Allah in Islam has no relationships. He can't be love. They never call him love. He can't be father because they say he has no son. Can you begin to see how the Trinity is precious to us? It is a vital part of our whole religion. God is love, he always was love, he always will be love. When there was no human being to love, he loved his Son, he loved his Holy Spirit, and they loved Him. And salvation is being invited into that family love. It is being brought in as an adopted son to share the love they already had in that threesome. Do you begin to see something bigger in this than just creeds and arguments? It is crucial. Thank God for the creeds that preserved the truth for us, because if they hadn't worked out those statements, we could have gone astray years ago. God is *the* Father, *the* Son, and *the* Holy Spirit – not three Gods but one God and Father of us all.

The next thing I want to say is that God, having made us in his image, has given us the pattern for our relationships with each other, and if you ask me why God created human beings, my answer is utterly simple: he already had one Son and one Spirit to love, and he found that that love was so pleasant and such a delight that he wanted a bigger family. And that is the reason why we are here – to be that bigger family. There is no other reason that you are here on earth except that. You are here to become God's adopted sons and daughters, part of his eternal love family. Therefore, among the redeemed, the Trinity is the pattern for how we live together. It sounds so obvious when you say it, but that is what Jesus prayed for. Jesus prayed for us who would believe on the Apostles' doctrine, and he prayed that we may be one as he is one with the Father. So the Trinity becomes the pattern for your relationship to the fellow believers in your church. Isn't that amazing? That the Trinity of love should be visible in the church. "See how these Christians love each other." That is how we will persuade the world about the Trinity, by demonstrating it among ourselves.

Can you begin to see the importance of the Trinity? The delight of it? Instead of regretting that you have to believe in the Trinity to be a Christian, you can rejoice that God is a Trinity and that therefore there is a pattern that has always been there, of how to live together. This applies to every thing as well as everyone. God's intention – his plan – was to bring all things together in Christ so that we might know the harmony he has already got, and that he has had for ever and ever. And he simply wants us to have the same harmony.

Could anything be simpler? That is how we can rejoice that we have got such a wonderful God, a God who *is* love, always *was* love, always *will be*, a God who wanted to share that love with us, and, above all, that he wanted us to share it with each other on earth and be a demonstration of the Trinity, and persuade others that people can be "one" in the best sense of the word. Only if we live in perfect harmony with our fellow Christians can we demonstrate the Trinity.

We adore the Trinity. We love the Trinity – and yes, Father, that you are what you are; that you are the great *I Am*; and thank you for showing us that you are a Trinity, three in one and one in three. How we love you. Help us to demonstrate that down here and convince other people that you are the Holy Trinity. In Jesus' Name. Amen.

I think there comes a time when you leave the questions behind and you say:

God, you are what you are, and you wouldn't be God if you weren't what you are, and we praise you, we rejoice in the Trinity. Amen.

ABOUT DAVID PAWSON

A speaker and author with uncompromising faithfulness to the Holy Scriptures, David brings clarity and a message of urgency to Christians to uncover hidden treasures in God's Word.

Born in England in 1930, David began his career with a degree in Agriculture from Durham University. When God intervened and called him to become a Minister, he completed an MA in Theology at Cambridge University and served as a Chaplain in the Royal Air Force for three years. He moved on to pastor several churches, including the Millmead Centre in Guildford, which became a model for many UK church leaders. In 1979, the Lord led him into an international ministry. His current itinerant ministry is predominantly to church leaders. David and his wife Enid currently reside in the county of Hampshire in the UK.

Over the years, he has written a large number of books, booklets, and daily reading notes. His extensive and very accessible overviews of the books of the Bible have been published and recorded in *Unlocking the Bible*. Millions of copies of his teachings have been distributed in more than 120 countries, providing a solid biblical foundation.

He is reputed to be the "most influential Western preacher in China" through the broadcast of his best-selling *Unlocking the Bible* series into every Chinese province by Good TV. In the UK, David's teachings are often broadcast on Revelation TV.

Countless believers worldwide have also benefited from his generous decision in 2011 to make available his extensive audio video teaching library free of charge at www.davidpawson.org and we have recently uploaded all of David's video to a dedicated channel on www.youtube.com

TAKE A LOOK AT YOUTUBE
www.youtube.com/user/DavidPawsonMinistry

THE EXPLAINING SERIES
BIBLICAL TRUTHS SIMPLY EXPLAINED

If you have been blessed reading this book, there are more available in the series. Please register to download more booklets for free by visiting **www.explainingbiblicaltruth.global**

Other booklets in the *Explaining* series will include:

The Amazing Story of Jesus

The Resurrection: *The Heart of Christianity*

Studying the Bible

Being Anointed and Filled with the Holy Spirit

New Testament Baptism

How to study a book of the Bible: Jude

The Key Steps to Becoming a Christian

What the Bible says about Money

What the Bible says about Work

Grace – *Undeserved Favour, Irresistible Force or Unconditional Forgiveness?*

Eternally secure? – *What the Bible says about being saved*

De-Greeing the Church – The impact of Greek thinking on Christian beliefs

Three texts often taken out of context: *Expounding the truth and exposing error*

The Trinity

The Truth about Christmas

They will also be avaiable to purchase as print copies from: **Amazon** or **www.thebookdepository.com**

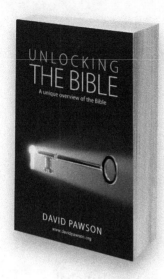

UNLOCKING THE BIBLE

A unique overview of both the Old and New Testaments, from internationally acclaimed evangelical speaker and author David Pawson. *Unlocking the Bible* opens up the Word of God in a fresh and powerful way. Avoiding the small detail of verse by verse studies, it sets out the epic story of God and his people in Israel. The culture, historical background and people are introduced and the teaching applied to the modern world. Eight volumes have been brought into one compact and easy to use guide to cover both the Old and New Testaments in one massive omnibus edition. *The Old Testament: The Maker's Instructions* (The five books of law); *A Land and A Kingdom* (Joshua, Judges, Ruth, 1&2 Samuel, 1&2 Kings); *Poems of Worship and Wisdom* (Psalms, Song of Solomon, Proverbs, Ecclesiastes, Job); *Decline and Fall of an Empire* (Isaiah, Jeremiah and other prophets); *The Struggle to Survive* (Chronicles and prophets of exile); *The New Testament: The Hinge of History* (Mathew, Mark, Luke, John and Acts); *The Thirteenth Apostle* (Paul and his letters); *Through Suffering to Glory* (Hebrews, the letters of James, Peter and Jude, the Book of Revelation). Already an international bestseller.

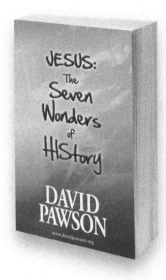

JESUS:
THE SEVEN
WONDERS
OF HISTORY

This book is the result of a lifetime of telling 'the greatest story ever told' around the world. David re-told it to many hundreds of young people in Kansas City, USA, who heard it with uninhibited enthusiasm, 'tweeting' on the internet about 'this cute old English gentleman' even while he was speaking.

Taking the middle section of the Apostles' Creed as a framework, David explains the fundamental facts about Jesus on which the Christian faith is based in a fresh and stimulating way. Both old and new Christians will benefit from this 'back to basics' call and find themselves falling in love with their Lord all over again.

OTHER TEACHINGS
BY DAVID PAWSON

For the most up to date list of David's Books
go to: **www.davidpawsonbooks.com**

To purchase David's Teachings
go to: **www.davidpawson.com**

CPSIA information can be obtained
at www.ICGtesting.com
Printed in the USA
BVHW040010221119
564505BV00003B/452/P